ADVANCE PRAISE FOR *AN HONEST WOMAN*

Perhaps only poetry can carry both the tremendous uncertainty
and the wisdom of being a woman? Most certainly, Jónína
Kirton's poetry bears the great undertaking of being a girl, a
daughter, a wife, and also a sister upon these unceded, ancestral,
and shared territories. Kirton's lines are spare and careful. She
recognizes the value of language, and the importance of a
reflective pause or breath. She knows the profound intention of
each and every word.

> —Amber Dawn,
> author of *How Poetry Saved*
> *My Life: A Hustler's Memoir*

In *An Honest Woman*, Kirton explores the complicity
and complexity of race, class, age, and gender relations.
Reproduction of harm, confusion of protection and
abandonment, rebellions that duplicate the status quo: these
poems steadily upend themselves, and together paint a
delicate sketch of our human condition.

> —Joanne Arnott,
> author of *Halfling Spring:*
> *An Internet Romance*

To read *An Honest Woman* is to step into a swirling tide of
memory and insight. Jónína Kirton offers us a gripping story,
set to the music of vivid poetry. We find ourselves – our
humanness – in her forgiving but honest account of how we
hurt each other, how we bear our broken hearts, how we love
and let ourselves be loved against all odds.

> —Oriah Mountain Dreamer,
> author of *The Invitation*

PRAISE FOR JÓNÍNA KIRTON'S PREVIOUS POETRY COLLECTION, *PAGE AS BONE – INK AS BLOOD*

A Bildungsroman in verse ... subtle, perceptive, and politically engaged.

—*Matrix*

These are poems out of a woman's experience and the matriarchy. Some of the most moving and affecting poems within the collection are love letters to the writer's/speaker's mother, who has died from breast cancer ... Kirton avoids outright confessional by raising the question of what voice is and can be, and does this as a poet ... introducing the awareness of human fallibility and how "story" is fraught, gives the writing authenticity, and the writer welcome authority. Moments like this in writing are hard won and as such are to be treasured and sustained.

—*The Maynard*

page as bone – ink as blood is restorative, intimate poetry, drawing down ancestral ideas into the current moment's breath. Writing from a place of "curious contradiction," "of skin a little wild," Kirton begins by re-spinning the threads of Indigenous immigrant, and poem by poem shoves the shuttle forward and back, remaking human integrity from ghosts and bloody matter. In these words, skin is not a barrier but a doorway through which the worlds stride. Kirton's poems are peacemaking, both generous gesture and much-needed literary poultice.

—Joanne Arnott, author of
A Night for the Lady

Jónína Kirton's memoir in verse could be an epic novel, a haunting ballad, a film noir. What it is: a visitation by ghosts and spirits, familial secrets, and retrieved historical mis-memories. As intermediaries between European and Indian cultures, she retraces her Métis inheritance and her own arduous journey to becoming a twenty-first-century guide we are much in need of.

—Betsy Warland, author of
*Breathing the Page: Reading
the Act of Writing*

Jónína Kirton sifts through her life – our lives – picking up piercing images and sorting stories of the senses, exploring the push-pull of being human, the delight and ambivalence of being in our own skin. Slowly, by being faithful to the moments, her poems find fragments of freedom by telling the truth.

—Oriah Mountain Dreamer,
author of *What We Ache
For: Creativity and the
Unfolding of Your Soul*

an honest woman

Jónína Kirton

Talonbooks

Talonbooks
278 East First Avenue, Vancouver, British Columbia, Canada V5T 1A6
www.talonbooks.com

First printing: 2017

Typeset in Bembo
Printed and bound in Canada on 100% post-consumer recycled paper

Cover design by Typesmith
Cover hand-lettering and interior design by Chloë Filson

Talonbooks acknowledges the financial support of the Canada Council for the Arts, the Government of Canada through the Canada Book Fund, and the Province of British Columbia through the British Columbia Arts Council and the Book Publishing Tax Credit.

LIBRARY AND ARCHIVES CANADA CATALOGUING IN PUBLICATION

Kirton, Jónína, 1955–, author
        An honest woman / Jónína Kirton.

Poems.
ISBN 978-1-77201-144-9 (softcover)

        I. Title.

PS8621.I785H66 2017   C811'.6

For Christine Hayvice

To note each other accurately; to be noted accurately: what we long for.

—Betsy Warland in *Oscar of Between: A Memoir of Identity and Ideas* (2016)

Contents

An Honest Woman

between

father daughter mother talks
never included race
unless an aside
your father hates being Native
or *comb your hair*
you look like a dirty little Indian
raised between two
later called a *Chink*
a *squaw*
squaw pants
one whose *mother*
chews moccasins
white trash
wannabe Indian
until mistaken
for local in Hawaii
next week on bus
white man says
why do you people
send all that money home
often asked
what are you anyway
fantasies of Indian princess
follow response
or lack of response
when spoken to in Spanish
until I between
mother   father
find alcohol
stumble in slush
along Portage and Main
hitchhike home
from disco
not knowing
"our women" go
missing

3

red light green light

blood the first betrayal
followed by tender buds
hard to hide
from foolish boys
who take delight
in punching potential

> from this she learns
> sometimes men
> do strange things
> with desire

bruised breasts   tiny tits
trapped in training
bra   the one she tried to hide

red light
green light nights
replaced
by dark basements
spin the bottle
with boys
once friends   now
sweaty with desire
they race towards
fantasy finish
but she is not
ready
offers
safe word shared
since childhood
red light

but he will not
stop
she screams
yellow light
but he will not
stop

devalued   within this hormonal frenzy
she becomes a place of release
and he   *the winner*   will never be *it*

who owns this body?

tongue hot, lips swollen
only cool water   iced lattes
bring some comfort

the energy healers say
there is   much   I am not
                              saying
my yogi friend said
it is the *rising*

                    kundalini energy

the doctor called it an

                                        acute infection

am I being attacked
        from the inside or   out?

dictionary says "acute"

                                        critical, crisis
the energy healers say there is much
        I am not saying   mind (critical)
                                        censors all I say
my yogi friend says
it is the *rising*
        kundalini energy (crisis)

stuck at the entry point
                    where nourishment
                                        enters my body

acute infection   at the delivery point, where
        my words spoken tell

                            the story of my life (critical)

the story my father would rather I   not tell
forty years later and he is still

                                        in my body

as I move closer (critical) to disclosure (crisis)
the pressure builds

                    — between us —

                                who owns this body?

he is nowhere near, miles away and yet
            my tongue explodes
                        just as it is about to tell (critical)
seeking closure   disclosure (crisis)
                                    it lets no nourishment in
kundalini rising, taking back
            what is mine (heat purifies)
                                will my words turn to gold?

doctor called it   an *acute infection*
I call it an invasion, a crisis (critical)
on my tongue, in my mouth the deliverer
                            of my messages
perhaps they are right, something has come
to the critical point
                the force (crisis)
                                behind it
                the need to tell (crisis)
                                to tell the truth (critical)
the momentum has built
is doing battle (crisis) in my mouth (critical)
                                with my father's need (for silence)

dispersed

Long before the body breaks down,
the spirit slips out inch by inch.

—Carolyn Myss
in *Defy Gravity* (2009)

at night she slips
into siren's skin
the disquieting type
it is a question of self-defence
her secrets remain   shadows
and he moulded hard
disciplined muscles
she a soft landing
consoled by small gestures
his mouth filled
with empty words
she wants   warmth
while he longs
to feel
her dampness
their bodies an occasion for contact
once finished
every night
they breath together
in darkness

sorry

peer-support training included
the honeymoon cycle
where I see my parents
the buildup towards a night of drinking
later screaming   hair pulling and more
and me crying   feeling mother's pain
        father's anger
next day confusion as lovers
take car rides together   hold hands
and me alone in back seat with thoughts of last night
question sanity of all involved

                        – until –

in grocery store
I must swerve
to avoid him buying bouquets of sorry
knowing later he will lay
flower offerings on my doorstep
followed by knocks
on all doors
all windows

most hot summer days
all openings are closed
or he will come in with the wind   whisk me
off my feet with his *come on baby* voice
which he often sends through mail slot
now taped shut
duct tape prevents his words
from entering

so many nights spent in darkness
sitting on plastic
footstool next to shower stall   all lights out
      waiting
for him to go
      waiting
for what comes next
phone calls   incessant

neighbour tells of late-night sightings
police alerted to his parking-lot surveillance

            no contact
          becomes order

first day at new job he is
on street corner   pulling
on sleeve

on way home he is
in back lane
must back up to avoid
his burgundy van
filled with memories
the others he harmed
never named but evidence of their presence
in his apartment that first visit
a forgotten scarf   the lipstick tube left on counter
that pink fuzzy sweater on armchair
he said they never came back
and I   like my mother
gazelle in wild dog's living room

dazzled by white-toothed charm
missed first clue
never questioned
why they never came back

wild dog at my door   I opened
and we entered the cycle I never understood
the buildup   screaming   hair pulling and more
next day drives in car with a man–child's broken heart
and we lovers   hold hands
my son in back seat   alone
with thoughts of last night
as he questions sanity of all involved

possessed

clogged for days   I try
writing with my left hand
some letters perfect
others oddly slanted
my home cluttered
my insides a muddle

clogged for days   I pray
while internal beavers chew the living
use what falls   to build dams
spend too much time with the dead
and this is what happens

possessions
how easily they accumulate
place themselves at the door   looking
for a way out
even they don't want to be here
their trail to the door includes
his empty envelopes strewn on floor
their blank stare part of his campaign to reclaim space
and every morning there is the water
all over bathroom counter

the dirty socks left on floor
all mini rebellions meant to stake
his territory
as my books   art supplies
stones   sage
threaten takeovers
daily I light candles
offer prayers and learn
to bless socks on floor
leave thoughts with water
on the bathroom counter

swallow

considers himself kind
as he places cool glass of water
on bedside table
this is not the Oval Office
but he does expect me
to swallow

he leaves behind
no blue-dress proof
all photos evidence
of a fun weekend at the lake
that was before
the gasping
his insistence that
all girls do this
for their boyfriends
but he is not my boyfriend
married man
a wife   children   at home
invited two young girls
to the family cabin
bring your bathing suits
we'll water-ski
it'll be fun

as plans were made
he never spoke
of his family
his intentions
that was until he had us
on his island
and there was no way home

mother father daughter talks

daughter becomes drunk
drives car
into pole

emergency room stitches (thirty-five)

                      lipsinsidemouthunderchin
later at bedside
mother sobs   *Why?*
father also drunk
says   *Shut up, Lorraine!*   *Shut up!*

to be female

how many times have I fallen
on the sharp edge of obligation
no one expects your husband to visit
the dying
no   this is
women's
work
your mother knew this
when she asked you to sit by her bed
in her final days
the bond of womanhood
a shared understanding
of need for one another

but I have no girls
who will sit with me?
as I begin the great disappearance

women without daughters   alone
others cast daughters aside.
female fetuses discarded   they wander
perhaps it is they who will gather
at my deathbed and we will
make the transition together

father's only daughter

a fish in water
she swam   fast
while he on sideline smiled
at her strength
but to her face
you are too independent
no one will want to marry you
his daughter   confused
by independence and need
for husband
soon learned
that men want
women with soft edges
fluid   supple   not swimmers
with strong backs
long arms that dig deep
into water   cutting cords
with men who want
women   dependent
like her mother   who cannot   leave

mother tries to teach daughter
to serve tea   to sell crafts
but doll clothes   doilies
frilly things
do not interest
daughter
who sees herself as alone
wolf in forest
where she seeks independence
out of sight of those who want
later in playground   alone
she claims the swings
the pumping of her legs
brings heat to her belly
that night skating
air crisp   fills lungs
as her legs
strong   steady   push across ice
father on sideline smiles
but will not say
good job, daughter! good job!

things I learned from my mother

a girl needs a good coat and nice shoes
there are recipes on soup cans
Campbell's knows how to feed a family
if your husband is faithful   a good provider
            be grateful
even if he hits you
            it is okay
as long as he is faithful   a good provider
never wear too much blush or you risk
looking like one of *those kind of women*
it is all right to have sex before marriage
as long as you have him over for dinner first
the recipes can be found on the Campbell's soup cans

a quiet thread

the river can be unforgiving
once it took my brother
my grief a quiet thread
became a tributary
filled with merciful rain
until my second brother did not drown
a bullet in his abdomen
created another tributary
a confluence of loss

overwhelmed by rush of water
I found myself susceptible
to sudden losses of consciousness
every morning I sank
my drowning
a daily consequence
quick   silent

but this morning
I wept at the joy of the sun
the way it creeps into every crack

black pearls

The climate in which feminine
sexuality awakens is nothing like the
one surrounding the adolescent boy.

—Simone de Beauvoir in
The Second Sex (1949)

black pearls on a string
when young lustrous
men dazzle yet frighten us
for many our first encounters
a plundering
the thread broken
and we all fall to the ground
roll away from one another
the descent begins
echoes of childhood become faint
arrayed   prepared   we flutter
we become the door that goes on opening
within us the place where everything converges
that *rupture with the past*
unexpected   brutal
sanctified and not sanctified
he stiffens like a bow   discharges
feminine flesh   prey   no pray
for these repercussions will be felt
for the rest of our lives

dispersed among men
without recourse   under siege
our body to be managed
a mystery to be conquered
a crest   a song
where *he surpasses himself*
while we must remain enclosed
our *body a situation filled with opportunity*

grab that pussy

I feel it so personally. And I'm sure
that many of you do too – particularly
the women. The shameful comments
about our bodies. The disrespect of
our ambitions and intellect. The belief
that you can do anything you want to
a woman. That is cruel. It's frightening.
And the truth is, it hurts. It hurts.

—Michelle Obama (2016)

women and girls everywhere
will not say
where it hurts

their bodies
war-torn countries
where between legs
we find
places of conflict
many try to hide in
bombed-out shelters
hoping to avoid
the daily losses of sovereignty

we know our flesh is considered
a place of entertainment
by man who says
I just grab them
by the pussy ...
and a whole country
that ignored whistles
from a dog
with a bone
picked clean
by toothy lies

while women wept
many alone in rooms

                     with others

who have never asked
where does it hurt?

suggestions of pivot
offered as possibility
that this man is not a monster
that we are in good hands
hands that grab pussies
and a mind that considers itself king
of castle   that looks for ways out
of fray caused by his own comments
    the rating of women
    late-night tweets
    assertions of non-existent Miss America sex tapes
when he is on tape
offering admissions of lurking
backstage with underage girls   naked
and fifty-eight years old when he speaks to Howard
about an eighteen-year-old
Lindsay Lohan saying …

deeply troubled therefore good in bed

so much recorded vitriol
and yet he will be king
showing us that the he-said-she-said
arguments are but smokescreen
we know what he said …
and it does hurt   everywhere!

mother father daughter future hubby

Father found at the Charleswood Pub. Drinks ordered. Four of us discuss wedding plans and I the blushing bride-to-be am happy to share this moment with mother, father, and my future hubby. Father, a regular, must have known what was next but gave no indication as the stage filled with a woman there to spread legs, twirl pasties. And I, unprepared, shake head, look around table for a sign that we should go. Father, future hubby are busy bonding over privilege and I stand up, turn to my husband, hiss words: *I am not staying here. Let's go.*

Mother grabs my elbow, pulls me closer, looks at father, whispers: *Don't embarrass your husband. Sit* DOWN!

I walk out.

Alone.

Welcome to marriage, daughter. Welcome!

dinner at the Clintons

in white pantsuit
she smiles
waves to the shouting
Hillary – Hillary – Hillary!
media flashes
to women
crying
some women
with many years
waited a lifetime
for this day

camera pans to Bill

daughter next to him

both watch mother
and I imagine dinners at the Clintons
campaign talk of polls
the way she   a woman
made honest by him
stood by
her man
while daughter learned
headlines burned
and my son only eight
at the time of the Oval Office
scandal
often repeated …

I did not
have sexual relations
with "that" woman

in darkness

a man kept his daughter captive
twenty-four years
behind eight locked doors
underfoot in the family home
her mother unaware
walked over
damp darkness
where four of her seven grandchildren
never saw
the sun   the others
left on her doorstep
note attached
father's little foundlings
daughter now vessel
mother says she never knew

daughter helped
carry the door that would close
only to open twenty-four years later
ether-soaked lungs
in chains until
metal gets in the way
mother's missing person

case soon closed by a note
father forced her
to write
to explain herself away

the authorities approved
grandmother   grandfatherfatherfosterparents
social workers make regular
visits   later learn
they had walked on
grounds and the family swam
over children below
no one heard
his mother in attic
windows bricked in
no sunlight for her either

there is no escape
from a son with a need
for a *second life*
who says
I was born to rape
and a lawyer who offers
in his defence
he is not a monster

a girl on the verge, New Year's Eve, 1967

> The sophisticated woman has always
> been the ideal erotic object.
>
> —Simone de Beauvoir in
> *The Second Sex* (1949)

ankles crossing and uncrossing mid-air
I lie on bed   watch mother lean
    into mirror   tilt head
apply eyeshadow
creamy champagne on lids
deep burgundy in crease of eye
splash of gold in outer corners
    ever so slowly she paints
black line around
already large brown eyes
followed by long strokes
Maybelline lashes
the perfect frame

brush of blush
on cheeks   chin   forehead
a final pat
powder to ensure
no shine
in photos
lips slightly open
she leaves a trail of red

leans away
from the mirror

                                        satisfied smile says it all

bra padded   pointy tits offer themselves
as she pulls tight
burgundy brocade
dress over hips
          long slit reveals silk legs
high-heeled   equipped with garter
in mirror stockings straightened

                                        she knows
                                        back seam
                                         invitation
                                        will excite

finishing touch   large
rhinestone brooch over
right breast
matching
earrings   dangle
will glisten
in candlelight   reflect her doe-eyed desire

flat stomach   thin body
remind me of a mature Twiggy

I cross and uncross my ankles
try to imagine myself   self-assured woman

          will I be like her?

years later her coaching includes reasons
why padded bra is necessary
for someone like me

cautioned against
too much
blush
long hair   (father likes it short)

most days I resisted her instructions
and now she is gone

I still have the brooch   the earrings
but   cannot bring myself to wear them
from time to time I take them out
                    hold them in my hands

                        they do glisten   sparkle still

too

as a child
often considered
too loud
too thin
later too fat
hair too long
skin too dark
makeup too much
too independent
the power of three letters
too   let's us know
there is a line
don't cross it
it is the crack
that will break
your mother's back

beauty tips 101

after my mother died I wore her nightgown
her wedding ring   having married her story
the shallow lies about beauty
        about pancake breasts
        the need for padded bras
how small pink nipples were better than mine
my lips too full   hers thin more appropriate
our hips   wide   will always require camouflage
beauty a smoke-and-mirror game that if played well
lands you the right man

surrender

falling leaves   compost
our falling   another matter
when we fall   whole worlds collapse
our children never expect
that they will have to pick us up
yet their turns come so quickly
like small children in need of rails to climb stairs
we are suddenly afraid of heights   *when did this happen?*
in our dreams we are still whole   wild and woolly
we scale walls   dance into the night with our sisters
in the morning   our body frail
its needs come in like a wave that has travelled
across an entire ocean to reach the shore
relentless   it pounds   the sounds
the force will push on us   until we agree to fall
once falling we find grace   there is hope in letting go
and eventually we understand

that letting go
is not giving up

the shoreline then becomes
a place of peace   of ebb and flow
where we find a new rhythm to follow
we discover our in-breath   our out-breath
has been deeply dreaming
will take us somewhere to float
will show us the way to be

in the rise and fall of it all

body sings

within my womb a song singing
a tadpole soon to be a boy
once you were born I found myself
still in need of somewhere to place my grief
and soon within my womb another song
tadpole soon to be a girl   an ally
but like all those Chinese mothers
I abandoned my daughter   released her
back into the pool of available souls

she tried again and again to swim upstream
but no one was there to greet her

we all know girls are hard to protect
and I tired of treading water

                        could not
                        hold her

let her drown   again and again
I tried once to join her
but he pulled me back
I could never abandon my son
overwhelmed by the water
of my own tears
I filled a bathtub
then a room
and eventually the world

coexistence

dark woods   deep songs   dream her
bones birds between words
she borrows time
                    chisels wood
      fills with water

while secrets nudge   some beyond words

nisîmis

I am the leaf of your childhood
pressed in wax   beside the buttercup
shone under your chin
I am the laughter once shared
with your brothers in the tub
three brown faces
hair pasted to your small heads
I am the fart in the tub
the bubbles no one wanted to claim
I am the swing in the playground where
you felt safe when alone
legs pumping until you merged with the sun
I am the popcorn ceiling you studied
head hanging
over the edge of the bed
as you prayed for your mother
I am the muffled scream in your throat
when they told you that your brothers had died

once considered a delicacy

i

I frequently hit black ice
do donuts until my colonized skin erupts
and I recall the way he pressed against me
breathed words heavy in my ear
do you have that tan all over?
as his hands sweaty-palmed their way
over bare shoulders
and I stuck between him and my till
must smile or lose job
all I can do is sigh   make note to self
do not wear sundresses to work

ii

transferred
to downtown
bank
where I count
money
draw attention   frequently
asked
what are you anyway?
followed by offers
dinner at Hy's
and a play
with stock trader
old enough
to be my father
(how bad can it be?)
at restaurant I am
offered a dish of disdain
from waiter
appalled
by my lack

I am not familiar
with
the way
waiters
huff   puff
over
questions of
boned
or deboned

later at play
still uneasy
I squirm
shocked
by unexpected
nakedness
as cast of *Hair*
full frontal sings

and he next to me
eager

I
am afraid

will not look
him in the eyes
cannot wait
to sink into my couch
stare at ceiling   breathe
a sigh of relief

iii

weeks later I try again
disco   dancing with the rich
more dinners at Hy's
I maintain distance
and the Jewish piano player calls me over
you don't have the pseudosophistication
that so many women who come here have
he hopes I never do
years later I realize
he wanted to say *run* …

iv

another presents himself at bank counter
with shaking hands   tremors of age
he stands at counter for everyone to see
two dozen large long-stemmed roses   red
with lust   he offers to set me up
my own apartment
and I blush   accept flowers but not offer
from this grandfather, father, and loving husband
who has need of me
is willing to pay

v

father always said
the bank is a nice job for a girl
but I decide to move on
to dining car
Via Rail takes me
Winnipeg to Vancouver
early warnings offered

by co-workers
manager must be kept happy
wide-eyed   willing
I do not understand
that this has nothing
to do with serving   food
that this man   large   sweaty
with kitchen grease   knocks
on sleeper-car doors
hopes to awaken
his sleeping beauties with a beer-filled kiss
first night I hear knocks
loud   stale   breath just outside door
I stay quiet
but next day he creates frequent opportunities
to brush up against
my tiny self
my mother's friend on train
pulls me aside to ask if I am okay
and I remember father's words

all waitresses are sluts

I don't want him to be right
so stop myself
from telling
say   *all is well*   wish
I had her number that night
when alone in strange city
there are many knocks
on hotel-room door
where TV gives me away

but I will not open
speak through crack only to say
I am tired from all that standing
still moving inside   seasick
from first train ride across prairies

once he leaves I sink
into couch   let out big sigh

                so many wanted access
                it stays with me even now

REDress

for Jaime Black

declared a day of mourning
for the missing
I hang REDress on my balcony
go outside to look for others
nothing   all balconies clear of red
so I walk the streets
hoping to find others
few know that I am one
of the "lucky ones"
raped   never murdered
only parts of me are missing
now sixty
I worry for the lost
for the "lucky ones"
aware that porn producer once said
every day another girl turns eighteen
so many bus stops   truck stops with one-way tickets
grief cuts bone
the daily dismemberment of our hearts
as our girls are manipulated
reported missing
and their loved ones left
to drag rivers in Winnipeg
while others walk highways of tears
where it has been said
you can feel
the spirits of the missing
and today in this city   on this day of mourning
their REDress arms empty
they wave to the cars that pass them by
on roadsides   on balconies
all reminders of what we are missing

truth

words ride bareback
potent seeds
they sprout
when watered
with our tears

your fish–hook words
barbed skin
too thin
roughening
considered necessary
preparation
for a harsh world
I'll give you something to cry about
once considered good parenting

spare the rod and spoil the child
granted permission
for the tag–team torture
at schools
in homes where
children should be seen not heard

your teachings say that your god
will forgive us all   one day
so why not lean in to the darkness

                                              darken others

reconciliation

how will I reconcile myself?
the Icelander and the Métis
the settler and the Indigenous
an ally to myself
since birth flung across a chasm
I often wonder am I to forever be
the way across
weak anchors at each end
my spine a flexible deck
load-bearing
and within my cables too much tension
as some try to cross
we all swing wildly
in each other's steps
without safety nets
the waves of emotion
threaten us all
and then there are times
that both sides seek to disown
to cut my cords
let me fall to the rushing
waters below
maybe one day I will just float away
see where the water takes me
but not today

today I will rebuild
this time no quick fixes   no steel cables
                    or wooden planks
no rust   no rot
no nails necessary
but rather the slow growth of twisted roots
from ancient trees
the way across a path
made of grandfather
grandmother stones
I will become a self-sustaining structure
gain strength over time
a living root bridge that lasts five hundred years

a holy hunger

Walking, I am listening to a deeper
way. Suddenly all my ancestors are
behind me. Be still, they say. Watch
and listen. You are the result of the
love of thousands.

—Linda Hogan in *Dwellings*
(1996)

my Homalco lover brushes
his long
straight
black
hair along my naked body
my drum belly pulsates
as the songs of his ancestors, my ancestors
and the music of the Métis merge

his horsehair bow against my body
how my fiddle frame vibrates
and from my throat I quiver

he is not my first Indigenous lover
for years I sought my culture via their scent
musky it merges with mine
and together we summon
the memories my grandmother tried to suppress
as her mind ran to the hills
our genetic scaffolding denied but not lost
the molecular residue unsettled
by my holy hunger for the truth
my "English" grandfather
was also Cree, Sekani   an English Métis
and my "French" grandmother
Chippewa, Nakota, and Ojibwa   a French Métis

for so long I sought her memories
in his Coast Salish body
a half-breed and an urban Indian lost
in this rainforest city
our ancestral lands miles apart
but still we found solace in each other
that tender act   the brushing of his hair
along my body, rare
for I was his booty call
the one he called once finished
playing pool at Joe's Café
once together we moved across
the territories of each other's flesh
unclaimed   we evoked memories of ceremony
our pow-wow skin a place our fingers danced

his calls for a little *sex therapy* always come late
but I never say no
even when he says
you fifty-cent pieces always marry white guys
I remain quiet
will not say
how much I want
to claim him
afraid my need
my loss of culture
will only further colonize us both

shadow of crow my crown

some days my mind a hollow place
where memories echo
my blood filled with the cries
of the ancestors   pulsates red
my bones the keepers
of their dreams for future
my hair devoid
of colour no longer sings
the songs of youth
my skin mottled
by age
still browns easily
my place in this city filled with uncertainty
and above movement   across sky
                    as many crows
                        follow me
from one streetlight to the next
their silent perching   unnoticed
until my neighbour points up
did you see all those crows?
they have been following you
down the street
I look up
shadow of crow my crown
ask   *what do they want?*
until I recall
it was just yesterday
that I asked
how does one keep in touch
with nature
in this city of noise
and today this shadow of crow my crown
follows me
down the street   home

mud mother

I am a mud mother
a dirty girl
I am earth
a birthplace
myth made alive   blood memory
walker between
worlds   familiar
with the great wandering
of water
I tap tap tap fingers on meridians
release rivulets of water just beneath skin
I want to live
to live as if
to live as if we are
to live as if we are of great interest
to live as if we are
of great interest
to the ancestors

idlenomore

there are words I wish I did not know …

fracking   nothing good can come of it
so why have it?
but then there are other words

fruit   filled with meaning
could be an apple and
where that takes us
a teacher – a teacher's pet
or forbidden   in the garden, naked

complexities arise
as we move through words
double meanings ask never to be pinned down
avoid all efforts at defining their desired outcome
even simple words like   *apple*
what they called "Indians" like me
red on the outside   white on the inside

indian car

within contained space of car
shared air   where cigarette smoke lingers
and coffee cup holders mucky with spillage
offer soy   sticky   smelly
they join in song with backseat garbage
chucked over right shoulder check
and yet I would never throw a candy wrapper
behind the couch
thinking I'll get it later

it's true I drive around town
in a large garbage can
one rarely cleaned
even though feelings of guilt
ride in seat next to me
held fast by seatbelt memories
of father's car
the duct-taped bumper
broken
mirrors
hanging
the taunts   *indian car*
which I quickly dismiss – my car is a compact

busy

the many emails chase her down the hall
while in the laundry room
she hears the to-do list shouting out deadlines
from the living room
and when she puts head on pillow
the unfinished blog posts begin to whisper
she hears *we are all storytellers*
and is tempted
to run to the computer
to chase after the words that want to be on that page
but she is too tired so drifts off to sleep
and eventually enters a dream
where the incomplete manuscript
hounds her
throughout the night

        nowhere is safe

even the plants have something to say
their little plant hands on their tiny plant hips
they weep for water
shake their little plant heads
the dishes in the sink have that look again
they have developed a dirty disdain for her
no one tells her that the vacuum is lonely
has begun talking to itself in another language
the broom and the dustpan
have organized a suicide watch

dark matter

> Human beings in all their
> complexity are seen as products
> of a molecular text …
>
> —Dawson Church in *The*
> *Genie in Your Genes* (2009)

it begins with DNA   essential
           for all known
forms of life
      repeating units
coiled around
      the same axis

transcription occurs
      a genetic mystery
filled with questions

                    I recall
               the therapist
                the words
        father   sociopath

cannot stop looking
      watching   documentaries
Most Evil
Born to Kill
as I investigate
      the minds
the lives of
those termed "evil"

             and I recall
             the therapist
             the words
     father   sociopath

in the documentaries
TV sound bites   newspapers
co-workers   neighbours   surprised
he was always so nice   a quiet guy really

again I recall
the therapist
the words
father   sociopath

in a universe filled
with dark matter
the little girl inside
still wonders
why me?

DNA the link
two strands
a double helix we share

even in death he will be with me

A Good Marriage

on her writing desk   pyrite
a masculine talisman of protection
some days she thinks only a fool
would dive daily for words
sink deeper and deeper into oceans
of inappropriate things they want to say

father wanted satellite daughters to circle his male planet
until pulled into the gravitational field of husband
once married   mounted again and again
asked to repeat *who's a bad boy now*
later expected to stencil flowers on walls
to macramé hanging plant holders
but what good are they   if she cannot grow
a single plant   her inadequacy mirrored
in wilted leaves and their refusal
to extend green offerings of assurance

she wants   loft apartment   small kitchen
all appliances functional but not overbearing
fridge filled with simple things
Honeycrisp apples and cheese
on the counter   black-olive baguette
not the white bread he desires
he wants ham   every Sunday
glazed with cloves holding pineapple tight
her Pyrex dishes and Tupperware-filled kitchen
a place of silent warfare

it's the small things in a marriage
the holding back   only to release in silence
the way he looks at other women
escapes to the garage   where he fondles trophies
creates shrines to his manhood

once finished   hours spent on porch
with cigarette companions   lighting one after the other
he swallows all resistance   fills with smoky stillness

her evenings begin with lavender
soaking in freestanding tub
and when alone   not a soap-opera viewer
        she watches horror
                hoping for clues
a way out of this Stephen-King-novel-of-a-life
she comes upon the notion
of an accidental death   offering a new life
a before-and-after marriage
but first

        she must ensure the life insurance has not lapsed
        that the children have finished college

until then

        she will be   a good wife
use the pyrite to guard against his control
create an inner symmetry that he will never notice
as she bakes apple crisp   smiles sweetly

irons his clothes
clears any clutter

        writes love poems to her future

I feel myself fall

petulant
through cracks
a flower
raised with little light
I keep poking up
through vitriol that is hate
having fallen
on my father's sword
the same sword used to gut him
fishlike learning
to breathe under water
in silence
I swallowed
he is a weather pattern
unpredictable
some days he provides warmth
the sun and a chance to grow
other days he considers my bloom
more weed than flower
but the bees don't care
still land
on petals made strong
by water   by wind

discarded

I once dated a homeless man
we met at the Friendship Centre
that evening he wore bone choker
deerskin vest   fringed
long black hair   wavy
bare chest   brown
leather pants
I thought I could feel the ancestors

or was it smell of suede
the Hollywood makeup?
he had been in a film that day   so bronzed clean
I could feel his spirit   strong   musky
within him a sinewy quiet
and when I closed my eyes I saw him

on a horse
on a hill

with others
arm raised

feathered coup stick in hand
he had touched many enemies
I prayed to know him

first date   he took me to English Bay
showed me the beech tree
its sprawling limbs provided

green shelter
          over grassy bed

he spoke of rain
when downpour comes
he walks
prays all night
a holy man in the city

next date he is in long black-leather coat
an extra in *The Crow* that day
not always clean   often hungry but
        he never complained
did not want a home   preferred to sleep
                outdoors
            under his beech tree

he had no phone but did call late one night
his arm broken   attacked by youth on Granville Street
I can still hear him   crying on the phone
my young son asleep in the other room

no, I cannot pick you up   no, sorry

        you cannot stay here

dating a homeless man is complicated
after dinner you leave him
on the corner   rain or shine
he walks away   and you hope
he stays away from Granville Street

water daughter fire mother

I was born of water.

                                  I know, dear. I was there.

What happens to a fire mother
when she has a water daughter?

                                  I think you know, dear.

All that water and your fire
in one home. I needed to float.
You needed to burn brightly.
Your daughter born an earth sign
with a watery chart grounded by
the hardness of the soil around me.
Even so I learned to flow with rivers and
lakes, to call the names of the Old Ones
when you, mother … you had Christ.

                                  I don't understand.

Yes, that's it. You never understood
that we inhabited different worlds.
Your losses, a burning fever
brought you closer and closer
to death. Mine, a weeping river
of grief, wound its way to another land.

                                  But, it was you who left first.

Moving to another province is not
the same as making a change of worlds.

                                  (*big sigh*) I was tired, dear.

I could never leave my son. You still had
a son, another water baby … He never learned
to flow, donned skates, sharp edges on frozen
water, he twirled, used a stick, a puck to score.

But what of your son, dear? An air sign …

Yes, with a watery heart, a mama's boy
his moon in cancer. A moon we share …

I would have liked to meet him.

Sometimes I think he is you. Is he?

I cannot say.

I understand … at least I think I understand.

Have you seen your father lately?

No … (*big sigh*)

I was born of water
with strong ties to this land.
You, mother, do you ever visit Iceland?

Occasionally I visit
my mother's spirit there.

The land of fire and ice. This we share …

Why does it matter to you, dear?
A mother always loves her child.

Really? Does a father always love his child?

I don't want to talk about that today ...

Was a curse placed upon us? The men
to be weeded out, two sons dead,
one husband burning in firewater.

You're always looking for reasons
when none are necessary.
What happens, happens.
Our dear Lord and Saviour
has His reasons, but
they are not for us to know.

Oh my God. Even my son's father
has abandoned him. You must know
they have never met. Is there a curse?
Is this a reckoning of some sort?

I don't know, dear.
Why worry about it ...
what can one do?

white space gone dark

on the altar an abalone shell filled with sage
leaning gracefully on blackened bowl an eagle feather
a few inches away a medicine bag
deerskin with a drawstring
inside the kinnikinnick and the sage I picked
some tobacco
all put together in a good way
a piece of driftwood, but what of the space between
there nothing   some would say
white space but it is black
matte, a bit dusty like an old breath
little attention paid to the space between
yet it is as important as all the items
carefully placed, one at a time
on the lid of my printer   a blank slate
where I decide to offer a place
for abalone shell   eagle feather
medicine bag   driftwood
to sit side by side
where they can offset printing
the mundane technical side of life

the sacred needs space
writing requires room   no cramming
no hoarding   no holding on
we must let go into the white space
allow sunlight to brighten page
bring memories
of days at the beach   skin touched by sun
sand washed away   at end of day
under covers, dark sets in   offers
a different kind of musing
a cave for our thoughts

where by candlelight
we write of the space between breaths   before touch
how longing lingers and words find their way to the page

darkness offers insights that
daylight's brightness cannot see

she sings

I sing the body electric,
The armies of those I love engirth me,
   and I engirth them,
They will not let me off til I go with
   them, respond to them,
And discorrupt them, and charge them
   full with the charge of the soul.

—Walt Whitman in
Leaves of Grass (1855)

looking over her glasses   new insights were found
      the kind that topple worlds
yet to many she seemed oblivious
            as she was often left without words

at night   a spiralling
in the moonlight   hands raised to the sky
            she praises the body
searches the stars for answers
            her feet on damp earth   wet grass between toes
arms outstretched she rocks   her full skirt swaying
gently touching legs   unshaven
with her whole body she sings   electric

in remembrance of love

we ask so much of memory   forgetting
                    it is a fragile thing
filled with corruption   mine and yours

we remember differently

the emotional content   the hard drive
some feel it is the software   but the body
    is not a computer
so let's stick to what drives the narrative
it is emotion   however it is stored
facts   dry material   assigned meaning
by how we feel about it all
these memories stored in cells fill us
with sadness   with love   and all
that goes between the two

there is no sadness without love
and no love without some sadness
my love for you   a wavering flag
half-mast   it feels the loss of you before you even leave
other times it flies high atop the flag pole
            pushing to and fro
as we explore each other's boundaries

time travel

for Bill Nighy

if we could go back and redo things
the many versions of our story would need
to find homes in parallel universes
where all our mistakes would hurl themselves
towards a future we hoped to avoid

would my father go back, save my brothers, my mother
or would he become that famous hockey player
accept that offer   five thousand a year   a try-out
with the Montreal Canadiens
would he finish the basement   find his way home
from the bar more often

would his fists only clench in the closet
where he would
imagine himself backwards
so he could move forward with ease
would he love me
give up firewater
or was his losing himself intentional
a call for death to ferry him to the other side

but it never took him   instead death
drowned his eldest son
as the firewater consumed more
of him   death came again
this time a fierce messenger
a bullet   ripped open
another son   leaving holes in us all

so he kept drinking
clenching and unclenching fists that knew flesh
until his wife began her descent
broken   her body rebelled
the black and blueness of fists against her face
the pain that pushed her down the stairs
        took more and more of her

no one tells you cancer smells of death
that love rots when too much is asked of it
but he could not keep her down
despite her pain there was always a lightness in her
I was there when she drifted away
no one tells you that those last moments of another's life
can change you   set you free

husband

raised on a farm
a father   a mother
two brothers   one sister
he is not the youngest
nor the oldest
towards the end   in the middle
in this story if he is the cat   I am the mouse
the mouse who played dead

thinning

for Jamie

you are thinning in every way
your hair falling away from your body
skin so close to bone
transparent it reveals
the pathways of veins
too slender for IVs
you were always delicate
my sweet nephew
and I have always loved
your ethereal nature but
this thinning   this fading too much
so I take shelter in your bathroom
hoping to collect myself

in mirror I see
many bottles of pills
toilet seat elevated   bathtub chair
usually signs of aging
but you are only twenty-five

this place of refuge filled with reminders of illness
the ache in my heart hurls me towards you
I try to stay close but you are leaving me
and I don't want to remember you this way
we are both caught in the riptide of loss
you know more than you say
and I find myself without words
cannot bring myself to offer empty reassurance
so together we sit in the silence that is your thinning

the death of love

it begins with a slight rumble
here and there
like thunder rolling
distaste   edges closer
anger's lightning rod scorches
the sender scarred   by their own words
by the disappointment wrapped in attempts
to reconcile but we all know that at some point
there will be no going back
the marriage bed a place of potential
often squandered by one
like the time your mother came to get you
when you found he had other lovers
and you could not get out of bed
she packed your stuff   took you home
to her burdens   two now drowning
in your father's love

today tears

water tumbles over ache
and still no one asks
where does it hurt?
each of us with our pain
bodies sealed shut
we will have denied ourselves
three times by sunrise

alone in our tombs of mourning
we lay upon stone slabs shivering
within these shrouds of loss
until comes an offer
to roll stone away
for the Marys to pray
to kiss our cheek
to bring our Lazarus hearts back to life

urban lovers

i am a door you have opened
a passage you have entered
i am a changing landscape
under your hand

—Joanne Arnott in "the high
meadow," *Halfling Spring*
(2014)

what will they say of us   the Internet generation
where romance lives in words and sex abides in photos
            our love untested by proximity
performance a dreamy prospect   as yet unconfirmed

many of us mark time by the clock
in the corner of the computer screen
not the rising and setting of the sun as we cross timelines
with the tips of our fingers on keys not bodies
careful assertions typed and retyped
before we press Send
the immediacy of the body lost – adrift
in a computer chair
lost in the web
forever searching
for that perfect One

I do know one who found her beloved
their inukshuk lover touched
by her tender words typed

full stop   no stop

sun earth water air

i

sand   white   hot
sun stokes   fire within

browns skin
   splashed
with water

wispy wind clears
      air dries
          skin   still

ii

      the wind with your hands   feel

        the sun   eyes closed

   yellow orange red

      skin loves it most

to hardwood floors everywhere

you were once a tree
everything in this room
was once something else
I was a petal in my mother's mouth
soft until made hard
you and I are not so different
our unfurling a jagged thing
each from a single seed
born of water we sprouted
I wanted wings but like you got limbs
once grown, you stretched tall
green fingertips reaching for the sun

while I lay on my bed
with echoes of last night
shouting in my ears
I stared at stucco ceiling

        while you outside   studied the sky

at the pool   in the tub   I am still one with water
while I floated   your roots dug deep
sought sustenance daily

our breath   once a symbiotic exchange
oxygen for carbon dioxide
how odd we should meet again in this yoga studio
where breathwork meant to relax
leaves me contemplating
this varnished version of you and wondering

        will we ever share air again?

every plant has a song

> All inanimate entities have spirit and
> personality so that mountains, rivers,
> waterfalls, even continents and earth
> itself have intelligence, knowledge, and
> the ability to communicate ideas.
>
> —Vine Deloria Jr. in
> *God Is Red* (1972)

too few landscape architects
  have a natural affection for plants
while the plants never think of themselves
as extensions of houses or buildings
complementary experiences
meant to pay homage
to architectural structures
  designers and clients participate
in the illusion of control
but some do want to know how things feel underfoot
that when allowed a chance to respond
plants themselves can create gardens

   that time is the ultimate master

set adrift in suburbia through mists
under cloudy skies soft pinks glow
chartreuses fluoresce ambers warm whites glisten

 lithe bunchgrasses wend their way down the path

a silent backdrop an organizing spine that anchors

the architect must orient the plant explore regionally
then suddenly a rogue tree windswept

   echoes the wild

shows off its special qualities

as light defines textures   a shallow slope
tender trunks to soften the effects of concrete structures
fluid associations   shifting contexts
and a conceptual frenzy
brings outcomes
loops of public engagement
a coalition of hard and soft elements

weathered stones at water's edge   an intimate respite
a seamless composition that brings acoustic interest
the cascading waterfall   a grand gesture

while arching oak branches encourage lingering
a narrow path invites a solitary adventure
leaving ample room for emergence

paths evolve   offer a place among plants
a rhythm that the eye can follow
the forest floor breathes death   decay   birth

some gardens are blessed   plants seed
            and distribute themselves
untamed replication   wildflower meadows   stone pots
not repeating lines of matching trees and shrubs
in some gardens plants have been allowed
            to have their own way
bold flowers mingle   grow next to the street
make a brief dependable appearance   year after year

the end

for my mother

mouth open
no words have left
those lips in a week
eyes closed
all sight turned inward
she is folding in on herself
I am to sleep
on cot next to her
awake all night
I watch each breath   wait
for last words
offer mine as prayer
penance for all that was not said
can she hear me?
each night I wait   watch
for a sign
that she still loves me
that she forgives me

I will rise ...

I create a tunnel nest of twigs from my life on sandy beaches
where the tide takes me out nightly   I long to be free
of this bondage   instead I sink deeper into its fleshy skin as its
serpentine body wraps itself around my wrists slipping its way
to my neck my mouth suppressing screams as it pushes its head
between my legs uses its reptilian body to create a chastity
belt of its grey flesh   there is an odd comfort that comes
with this beast between my legs   the familiarity we enjoyed
as children remembered   I have seen the devil   the one
whose name we shall not speak   he has lived in the eyes of
my father but only when firewater took over his body – I am
my father's only daughter – a dark horse marked at birth passed
from man to man I learned too early that he was right – I do
not know the world of men – but what he and the others
cannot see is that I can shed my skin   leave this beast with
my unnecessary flesh   a shape-shifter   I am a bird by day
fish by night – I have been here forever and I will rise again
and again ...

Acknowledgments

Writing poetry is for the most part a solitary endeavour, often done in the silence of a bedroom or sitting on a comfy couch. Even if done in a coffee shop, there is a cordoning off; a movement away from the mundane world takes place. Once finished, we have a rough draft and, if we are lucky, we have a first reader. In my case that is my husband, Garry Ward. We often debate the merits of changing a word, a line break, or whether a comma is necessary. Our discussion always brings insight and frequently his observations or suggestions greatly improve a poem. Thank you, Garry.

I find the writing exhilarating, but the revising and editing – not so much. There is always a lot of hand-wringing, which I have come to accept as part of the process. I am so grateful for the patience of those who walked with me during this phase.

This book has been in the editing arms of a number of women who I greatly admire. Shazia Hafiz Ramji's insightful questions and kind attention brought forth new pieces that filled in gaps and made this a much more cohesive collection. Betsy Warland offered gentle guidance on a few pieces that I had difficulty completing. I have worked with Betsy so much that she practically lives in my head. I carry her and her word wisdom in my heart. And then there is the hand-holding that Ann-Marie Metten provided. She is so much more than just an editor. Also a friend and neighbour, Ann-Marie provided the kind of support I really needed to move through the editing process.

Once again Les Smith provided an excellent cover. As usual, I had something else in mind, but when I saw what Les came up with, I was sold on his design. Many thanks to Les for his willingness to provide options.

Since joining the pool of Talonbooks authors, I have had the pleasure of working with Spencer Williams. He walked me through my first book release by providing coaching tips on readings and so much more. Chloë Filson always has a smile for me when I show up at the office. I have so appreciated the ongoing support of Vicki Williams and Kevin Williams, who have welcomed me into the Talon family. I could not ask for a more supportive publisher.

Earlier versions of some of these poems have appeared in other publications. Thanks to the editors of *Humber Literary Review*, *The Litter I See Project* (thelitteriseeproject.com), *Room Magazine's No Comment Project* (roommagazine.com), and *The Science of Poetry, The Poetry of Science* chapbook (print and online at aileenpenner.com).

There are so many more that I could thank. I hold my hands up to those who sat in writing circles, took long phone calls, and entered into Facebook chats. So many listened as I lamented the painful process of writing a collection of poetry that cuts so close to the bone. Others provided inspiration through the sharing of their own stories. I will say their names here (forgive me if I have forgotten anyone) ...

Senator Lillian E. Dyck
Chelene Knight
Kelly Roulette
Susan Deer Cloud
Oriah Mountain Dreamer
Karen Davis
Sharon Jinkerson-Brass
Ingrid Rose
Sylvia Taylor
Joanne Arnott
Carleigh Baker
Amber Dawn
Michelle Sylliboy
Renae Morriseau

...

Notes on the Poems

black pearls was inspired by Simone de Beauvoir's *The Second Sex*, and the poem contains lines taken from her chapters on sexual initiation and adolescence. In fact, it was her book that sparked the idea for this entire collection of poems. As I read de Beauvoir's words, I became increasingly angry about my own adolescence; not only the violent start that many of us experience in "sexual initiation" but also that women are not encouraged to find what pleasures them. Yet as evidenced by the proliferation of teen porn, teenage girls are the objects of gratification for many men. As young girls we find ourselves in a hormonal soup that often diminishes our own budding sexuality, while boys are encouraged to explore, to not take no for an answer. And as young boys try to have their way with us, older men want to dominate. Their eyes are on us everywhere we go. At no point are we encouraged to have sexual agency. We learn to live within the male gaze and to situate ourselves in the power dynamic that exists between us and men. We are to be "good girls," to say no, to be attractive but not too attractive. The fact that de Beauvoir's book was written in 1949, yet still so much applies to young woman and their sexuality today, left me pondering. How can we change this? How can we support young women in finding their way in the world of sex and pleasure when so many still consider this to be a man's domain? When slut shaming is so prevalent and women's bodies are but a means to an end, where will women's sexual agency come from? I believe it lies in education. Both boys and girls need to know sex is normal and healthy and it is not, as many religions and societies have deemed, the territory of men.

grab that pussy was clearly influenced by the goings-on in the U.S. election and was written during the campaign. To witness the reaction to his words, *I just grab them by the pussy*, and to see that this and all his accusers could be ignored, that he was going to be the president of the United States of America, was a triggering event for me and many other women. Writing is my way out. I write to reclaim territory. To say *hell no* … We are watching.

dinner at the Clintons was inspired by Hillary Clinton's nomination as leader of the Democratic Party, an incredibly exciting moment for many women. The frequent camera shots of Bill in the audience brought thoughts of his Oval Office scandal. As I watched him and their daughter, Chelsea, I could not help but wonder what they discuss at family dinners. Clearly they are a political family and Chelsea is a very wise young woman. How does a daughter survive such a public discussion of her father and his Oval Office blow jobs? What did she learn when her mother chose to *stand by her man*? What did this cost Hillary in terms of her political career? No judgment. Just questions. This poem is simply another mother-father-daughter triangle as seen throughout the collection.

in darkness is about the Fritzl case. Since being told my father was a sociopath (as noted in *dark matter*), I have had a fascination with other fathers deemed dangerous – though I have long since dismissed the assertion that my father fit the criteria for this personality disorder. Regardless of any label that might apply to him, what is clear is that he was a danger to his wife and children. The mother's role in these situations is something that I am still sorting through, so the impetus for the poem was the nagging thought that, as a mother, I cannot imagine walking on the floor over a room where my missing daughter lived for twenty-four years. How could she not have known? But then I recall the ways in which my father gaslighted my mother.

These are complicated matters with no simple answers. That some fathers harm their children, that some mothers turn a blind eye, is undeniable. The reasons for all this are beyond my understanding at this time. It haunts me that anyone could do this kind of harm to their daughter. It hurts to know that so many mothers feel powerless to protect their children. I write of this story to note the brutality that exists out there.

While I hate to see men like Fritzl gain any kind of infamy (after his arrest, Fritzl boasted to a reporter from Germany's mass-circulation *Bild* newspaper that he was "world famous"), I do feel it is important to bear witness to these atrocities, to remember the women and children affected by men like him. The interviews and archival footage in David Notman-Watt's documentary *Monster: The Josef Fritzl Story* (2010) reveal that these monsters walk among us. As explored in *dark matter*, these men can be our neighbours and friends.

nisîmis means "my younger sibling" in Cree. Losing my brothers in their teens shaped my life in ways I am still sorting through. This poem is included in this collection because the heavy drinking and promiscuity in my twenties was in part my way of escaping the pain brought by their loss. I adored my brothers and they adored me. Losing them made me even more vulnerable. When no one greets us and our pain, open-armed, we must find a way to close. For a time, alcohol and men were a reprieve, a way to close off from the world. This poem is my opening back up to the wonder of a childhood shared with two sweet boys who are no longer with us.

REDress was inspired by Jaime Black's installation art project, "an aesthetic response to more than 1,000 missing and murdered Aboriginal women in Canada." One cannot discuss violence against women and not include the murdered and missing Indigenous women. When I began my healing more than thirty years ago, one thought lingered. Had I been subjected to "special attention" from men who thought "squaw" when they looked at me? I once brought this up in a therapy session and my concern was dismissed. What I think I heard was "I don't see you as Aboriginal so why would that matter?" Yet when out in the world I was constantly asked by men "What are you anyway?" Clearly they identified me as an exotic Other and this, combined with my father's rejection of me, did make me more vulnerable. Too often well-intentioned people dismiss important revelations. As women, we need to learn to trust our instincts. It is our best protection. There is no question that Indigenous women are targeted more often than non-Indigenous women. The statistics do not lie. The situation is shameful and leaves me and many others with a burning anger, a deep sadness that has nowhere to go. The REDress project, with its visually compelling, empty red dresses, was an impactful statement that travelled the country. I give thanks to Jaime Black for bringing forward this artful response to this ongoing tragedy.

In *truth*, "words ride bareback" – how I love this phrase but cannot lay claim to it, as these are the words of a dear friend, Carol Harmon, used with her permission. I first heard it in one of Ingrid Rose's *writing from the body* workshops. It was in a poem Carol wrote, and she used it in an entirely new way. What I heard was "words without condoms," "bareback" meaning sex without protection. Not safe. Maybe not even welcome. This seemed a fitting way to begin a poem about the truth of child-rearing tactics brought to Turtle Island by the settlers and used in residential schools, where sexual abuse was rampant and words were often weapons. No protection found in those times.

a holy hunger are the words of my dear friend, author and storyteller Oriah Mountain Dreamer. This poem has been shared with its subject and he has granted permission to use his words.

mud mother speaks to the need for connection with the earth and the ancestors. The ending comes from something I think I once heard … *We should live as if we are of great interest to the ancestors*. I have been unable to trace the source. It was one of those teachings that stayed with me and has been making its way through my awareness as I attend to the call of those who have gone before. Like many good teachings, it takes time to reveal itself. I am still learning to live as if I am *of great interest to the ancestors*.

indian car is a term I heard frequently growing up – they are now referred to as *rez cars* – used to describe big, poorly maintained boats often filled with smiling, brown faces. In my day, back-seat adventures included hanging out the window and lying on the shelf in the rear window.

As a child, the terms *Indian car* and *drunk* or *dirty Indian* lived in my head. They hurt my spirit. I thought about them when looking at my dad, who took three showers a day. I wondered if he feared being "dirty." It appeared that he and most of my Métis relatives did indeed take special care with their appearance and their homes, which had to be spotless. Respectability politics loomed large and everyone policed each other. I knew what the world thought of us *Indians*, and it pained me to think that anyone would say those things about my dad, a Métis man who took great pride in his appearance yet whose car was always dirty and in disrepair. In fact, the last time I saw his car, it was parked sideways in his parking spot (no doubt the result of a night of heavy drinking), with many dents, the side mirrors hanging by cords, and the bumper duct-taped on one side. The shame of being the daughter of not only a *drunk* but a *drunk Indian* rose in my chest until I pushed it away.

This poem reclaims this disparaging commentary on us and our cars, and it brings forward the fact that even young children are aware of subtle and not-so-subtle slights directed at them and their families. These things hurt and have a way of staying with you. Some days the pain is so great that I must write about it, and at times I feel the need to end with a joke or by poking fun at the very things that were intended to harm us. Hence the ending … *my car is a compact.*

In *busy*, "we are all storytellers" is a quote from an interview I did with Renae Morriseau while she was the storyteller-in-residence at the Vancouver Public Library. Renae has been a creative and healing force in our community. I hold my hands up to her for she has a generous spirit and has made me and many others feel welcome in the Indigenous world.

A Good Marriage was inspired by the Stephen King novella and movie with the same title. **Spoiler Alert**: I was struck by the way Stephen King seemed to be able to enter the world of a traditional wife who discovers her husband is a serial killer and has to figure out what to do with this information. Her response was compelling. Aware that the wives and children of serial killers are marked for life, she took time to explore her options. Like many women, she had to stay safe by not tipping him off. This meant having sex with a man who she not only despised but also feared (something hinted at in another poem, *dispersed*). While I hated to see all the victims and their families left without closure, I was thrilled to see King provide a believable story that broke free of the helpless-wife narrative. He did this in a very creative way ... one revealed in the poem at the end.

discarded is about a man who remains very important to me.

time travel was inspired by the movie *About Time* (2013), featuring Bill Nighy as a time-travelling father. This may be one of my favourite movies ever (but then I am a huge fan of Bill Nighy). The film shows us the vulnerability of being a father; that fathers make mistakes they would correct if they could. It made me wonder what my father would have done if he could go back in time.

In *today tears*, "where does it hurt" was taken from one of my favourite poems, "What They Did Yesterday Afternoon," by Warshan Shire. What to do with all that pain?

every plant has a song is a found poem of sorts. The title is taken from *Relatives with Roots* by Leah Dorion. Most words and phrases are taken from books on landscape architecture by Kelty McKinnon and Scott Ogden and Lauren Springer Ogden. This poem was part of a project organized by Aileen Penner, who gathered five poets and paired them with four scientists and a landscape architect. The non-poets shared their work with us; some even took their poet to work. In turn, the poets taught them a little about poetry and then we all wrote poems that were published in a chapbook and performed at the launch. I was paired with an amazing landscape architect, Kelty McKinnon. For my poem I took the language found in landscape architecture texts and used it in a subversive way. I believe plants have agency. That every plant does have a song. So while I appreciate the beauty that landscape architecture can bring us, I do like what nature offers. In other words, the way things go on without us.

Sources

Joanne Arnott. *Halfling Spring: An Internet Romance.* Neyaashiinigmiing, ON, and Owen Sound, ON: Kegedonce Press, 2014.

Simone de Beauvoir. *The Second Sex.* Translated by H.M. Parshley. Harmondsworth, U.K.: Penguin, 1949.

Jaime Black. The REDress Project. Art installation in public spaces throughout Winnipeg and across Canada. REDress.org.

Dawson Church. *The Genie in Your Genes: Epigenetic Medicine and the New Biology of Intention*, 2nd ed. Fulton, CA: Energy Psychology Press, 2009.

Vine Deloria Jr. *God Is Red: A Native View of Religion.* Golden, CO: Fulcrum, 1972.

Leah Marie Dorion. *Relatives with Roots.* Translated by Rita Flamand. Saskatoon: Gabriel Dumont Institute, 2011.

Linda Hogan. *Dwellings: A Spiritual History of the Living World.* New York: W.W. Norton, 1996.

Kelty McKinnon, ed. *Grounded: The Work of Phillips Farevaag Smallenberg.* Vancouver: Simply Read Books / Blueimprint, 2011.

Renae Morriseau. "We Are All Storytellers." Interview with Jónína Kirton. *Room Online.* roommagazine.com.

Caroline Myss. *Defy Gravity: Healing Beyond the Bounds of Reason.* Carlsbad, CA: Hay House, 2009.

Aileen Penner. *The Science of Poetry, The Poetry of Science.* Vancouver, 2012. aileenpenner.com.

Michelle Obama. Speech at a campaign rally for Democratic nominee Hillary Clinton presidential campaign in New Hampshire, October 13, 2016. Full transcript released by the White House Office of the First Lady, Washington, DC.

Scott Ogden and Lauren Springer Ogden. *Plant-Driven Design: Creating Gardens That Honor Plants, Place, and Spirit.* Portland: Timber Press, 2009.

Betsy Warland. *Oscar of Between: A Memoir of Identity and Ideas.* Halfmoon Bay, BC: Caitlin Press, 2016.

Warsan Shire's poetry and words can be found on warsanshire. blogspot.com and warsanshire.tumblr.com.

Walt Whitman. *Leaves of Grass.* Brooklyn, NY: n.p., 1855.

Jónína Kirton
is a prairie-born Métis/
Icelandic poet, author, and
facilitator. She currently
lives in Vancouver, on
the unceded territory of
the Salish people. Kirton
graduated from Simon
Fraser University's Writer's
Studio in 2007 and is a
member of its Advisory
Board as well as the
liaison for its Indigenous
Advisory Board. Kirton is
also a member of the *Room
Magazine* editorial board.

In 2016, Kirton received the City of Vancouver Mayor's
Arts Award for an Emerging Artist in the Literary Arts category.
Nominated by her mentor Betsy Warland, Kirton is excited to
be Warland's apprentice at the 2017 SFU Writer's Studio. Kirton
also won first prize and two honourable mentions in the Royal
City Literary Arts Society's Write-On Contest in 2013 and an
honourable mention in 2014 in the Burnaby Writers contest.

Kirton's work has been featured in a number of antholo-
gies and literary journals, including the *Humber Literary Review*,
Ricepaper Magazine (Asian/Aboriginal Issue), *V6A: Writing from
Vancouver's Downtown Eastside*, *Other Tongues: Mixed Race Women
Speak Out*, *Pagan Edge*, *First Nations Drum*, *Toronto Quarterly*, and
Quills Canadian Poetry Magazine. Her first collection of poetry,
page as bone – ink as blood, was released to wide acclaim by Talon-
books in 2015.

Photo: Ayelet Tsabari